Poems Only A Mother Could Love

Sarah Jacobs

BookLeaf
Publishing

Presentation by *BookLeaf Publishing*

Web: www.bookleafpub.com

E-mail: info@bookleafpub.com

ISBN: 9789357440844

First edition 2023

This work is dedicated to a determined eight-year-old who would be delighted we got our writing published, and to an angry twelve-year-old who would be annoyed it took this long.

ACKNOWLEDGEMENT

I want to thank my family for supporting my book hoard, my friends for enabling my ego, and my old English teacher who taught me that poetry doesn't have to be good to be published.

PREFACE

These poems were written at 3 am in a phone's notes app, under the assumption they would never be viewed. The writer humbly extends her apologies to any readers under the misapprehension that she has talent, creativity, or anything interesting to say. Instead, she invites you to remember that poetry, first and foremost, is about reading something written by another person and going 'hey...me too.'

The Worst Poem

This is the worst poem ever written
I am sure of it
I shall have no fanciful metaphor
No lyricism wrapped in prose
The rhyming scheme is completely off
And the rhythm is a bit on the nose
I shall not remember how
To make the audience empathise with the writer
Because when the writer cannot empathise with
herself
How could she expect it of the reader?
And really isn't the point of poetry
To speak from the heart
(I'm not sure I have one)
So instead QUICK LOOK
...sorry that didn't go anywhere
I shan't try to distract you again
From the fact this is the worst poem ever
In fact, I'll say it again

There is no colourful language
No descriptions of a wine-dark sea
And I'm certain that once this is over
You'll not think a poet of me

No, this poem shall be the worst ever written
But I can guarantee you this
No matter how badly this poem is written
The world is better it exists.

Letter Grade

3

All's well that ends well
Because grades don't really matter anyway and a
pass is a pass but I
Can't believe this my mom is gonna kill me and
I
Definitely don't belong here what on
Earth was I thinking there was no way I could
do anything but
Fail

Rhyme

Cannot I tell a poem without
First concocting a rhyming scheme
So brilliant it makes compare to
Those of far more notable a talent but
To first speak of my anger I
Must first make it palatable for
How else will you understand if I am not
Entertaining
I scream into voids and
Have a list of injustices burned into
My flesh that I flinch
To touch but you
Cannot understand my
words unless I make them
Rhyme

In Defense of Love

5

In the case of love, your Honour
I have come to the conclusion
That only that between Adam and Eve
Is deemed worthy of inclusion
That the only time you find love to be true
And of a most respectable cause
Is when it comes from what you view
As fulfilling your natural laws

What happens next, your Honour
For people whose love is different
Is we are taught to hate ourselves
By the vicious and the ignorant
For you see it's just a phase
A mere "season of confusion"
We cannot know what we really want
In a word- delusion

How can you call us equal?
When all you teach is shame
Speak only in euphemisms
Of the love you dare not name
I cannot say with truth your Honour
That I find prosecution just
That they can demand evidence of love

Else be doubted for common lust

Would you have me stand in the dock, your Honour
Place sinners hand on sainted tome
Speak truth plainly in open court
Of the love I dare to own
Enter into evidence my traitor's heart
Rip her beating from my breast
As though she could prove me worthy
Of the dignity I request

I cannot present my heart to you
For you see I gave it whole away
I traded it with a smiling girl
Whose gaze I caught one day
I later threw it to my closest friend
Who thought it were a game
I picked it up and dusted it off
And promptly lost it again

So you see, your Honour
My heart isn't available to weigh
I gave it to my sweetheart
And with her it will stay
But furthermore your honour
If you do not think me bold
Why must I be taught of shame?
Why can't our stories be told?

Therefore I ask you, your honour
Whatever your judgement be
Is any life worth living
When denied the right to be free?
So thank you, your Honour
I will end only on this
If I am to be damned
Let me end it with a kiss

Storm

No one ever says what happens when it gets
better
When your boat sails through the storm
How to go back to a life
Where you're cuddled up safe and warm
How you never stop jumping at thunder
Even tucked into your bed
And how even the kindest of words
Get all twisted in your head
The shadows retreat into ghosts
That haunt you through the day
But you can't talk to anyone
Since they think the shadows a-way
They can't know that it took you three hours
To be brave enough to show your face
How you're scared that they will notice
You don't fit into this space
The fear and the pain it forged you
Created who you are now
And while you'd love to let go of the storm
You've realised you don't know how

Maria Goretti

Maria Goretti was the Saint I chose
When the time came around to pick
They gave us a big book of saints' names
To help see which one would click
I flicked past Assisi, past Joseph, past Paul
The pages flew past in a whirl
For I knew the right one for me
Would have to be a girl
Eyes glazed past Saint Mary, Teresa, and Kate
Their names printed neatly in line
Then along came Maria Goretti
And her age was so close to mine!
I had made my choice and proudly wrote
Her name right after my own
I didn't consider it taking
Her name was merely on loan
But now I'm older I view with dismay
That poor girl whose name that I took
She didn't deserve to have something else stolen
By a girl picking saints from a book

Miss You

I thought about you yesterday
While washing dishes in the sink
There are flowers in the garden now
In shades of blue and pink

I thought about you yesterday
Whilst hoovering the stairs
And how they say that sometimes
Souls are born in pairs

I thought about you yesterday
And the day before
I thought how happy you'd be for me
And cried a little more

I thought about you yesterday
And I'm pretty sure it's true
If things carry on this way
I will tomorrow too

My Monster

My monster is the quiet sort
They do not growl or hiss
They instead speak to me softly
Of all the things I miss

My monster is the inquiring sort
The kind to go out of their way
They often ask in a confused tone
If anyone cares what I say

My monster is the cunning sort
They really are quite smart
They know just what to say to me
To completely break my heart

My monster is the caring sort
I really can't complain
They remind me that I should not try
I'll only fail again

My monster is the hiding sort
That only I can see
Every time I look in a mirror
They stare straight back at me

The World Screams

The world is a silent scream
It shakes the very ground
There cannot be a more terrifying
Absence of a sound

The world around us is quaking
Shaking, faking, forsaking
A noise so terrible no one noticed
the sound that it was making

The world inside is quiet
Hardly a squeak was heard
Never was so much said
With not a single word

The world without is screaming
Their cries rattle the shelves
But those on the inside cover their ears
For it's every man for themselves

Am I Gay Quiz

Am I...
tap, tap, tapping keys
The search bar blinks serpent slow
as it offers me
an apple dangling which
promises answers just out of
reach that I should not stretch out and
touch
I click the first option then flinch at the glare of
colour coming from
My phone at 3am (why am I awake?)
The questions are simple (definitely a trick)
And a version of me answers who keeps her
heart locked in irons but
No.
It is 3am and no soul is awake but me and the
snake
Refresh
Try again.

A
B
A
A
C

Does A mean something? Was I born answering
A or did watching the Disney channel as a child
warp my brain to like-

Done.

Oh.

Shit.

The life experiences of the old oak tree (As told from the perspective of a squirrel)

Whilst sitting amongst the leaves
I cannot help but wonder
The story of these eaves
Which leaves me now to ponder
Was this giant always here?
Vast trunk and dizzying height
Were the skies before clear?
Did branches always block light?
Perhaps once this giant was small
Smaller than even me
Perhaps before there was nothing at all
For there were no eyes to see
Or did this God appear one day?
From nothing to shades of green
Is that just a giant's way
Could this have been foreseen?
But what does a squirrel know of
What things could have been
Does it really matter though
How the universe came to be?
As far as the squirrel knows
There's always been a tree

First Sign Language Class

Hello!

My name is, no wait sorry,

Hello name me,

Oh that sounds weird
My fingers shape these familiar foreign phrases
which a self-depreciation learned from too many
times not showing perfection
But to carry on

Hello!

A smile is needed for this, tone is important and
you want them to like you please let them like
you but first you must get your hands to shape
words they know but do not yet understand, like

Name

Two fingers leave the forehead with more
enthusiasm than needed

Me

Who is that anyway to define self with one hand
seems impossible and yet

What

Exactly, what is going on what did you sign up
for this for did you really think you could just
raise your hands and suddenly understand, a
whole world at your fingertips but

The instructor smiles, and raises their hands to
answer.

One Time I saw Jesus in Asda

One time I saw Jesus in Asda
I don't think that he saw me
He was perusing the bread and wine
Located in aisle three

He helped an old man load up a cart
Of ready meals just for one
And spoke softly of how those we love
Are never really gone

I looked for him in church
But all that I could find
Were strangers reading scripture
To those who were left behind

One time I saw Jesus in Asda
Stood patiently in line
He carried a reusable bag
Which sort of looked like mine

He spoke of love thy neighbour
And to everyone be kind
I'm not convinced I could do that
For mercy is hard to find

Later I went to the temple
I thought that I'd find him there
But instead I only saw paintings
And couldn't bring myself to care

So I find faith in all the small things
Prayers written on shopping lists
For how else can I find meaning in the world
When I'm not really sure it exists

Stranger in the Mirror

Every day I look in the mirror
I have to avert my eyes
For you see my bathroom mirror
Is prone to telling lies

Well it may not be the mirror's fault
My reflection isn't right
What wrong could be done by glass
That only reflects the light?

The problem with my reflection is
My body is not mine alone
For, somehow, along the way
It gained a life of its own

Before, we worked well together
Did everything as a team
But now I look at myself in the mirror
And wonder what it could mean

That the face peering back at me
I hardly recognise
Whilst her face may look the same
It is clearly a disguise

The girl looking back is happier
Than I've ever been before
She smiles at me quite cheerfully
It shakes me to the core

Who could this person possibly be?
This smiling masquerade
I think she may be here for good
I've never been more afraid

i hate spellin

bekaus the words leaf
my brian too fast to
be constrayned to one
way of righting down
the contents off wishs and
feavered kreations for how kan
tumbiling dragones and towerring
spires that reech hih into vortexs beeyond
imaganation be constraned
to such a stagneet forme?
 tyed down to
just one thing as though it was not
imaganation that first thought of
words so reely what came first the
speeling or the dreame?

3 am Honesty

I wrote this poem at 3am
Curled up tight in my bed
Doing my best to quiet
The war raging on in my head

I wrote it down in my notes app
The screen light hurting my eyes
As I tried to work out the best way
To explain that it's all a disguise

That my smile was practiced twice weekly
The real one I do well to hide
And my eyes will never quite meet yours
They will glance off just to the side

I don't understand language
Especially turnings of phrase
When I was told it rained cats and dogs
I watched the skies worried for days

To step in your shoes I'm afraid
I can only literally do
But the leather feels too tight and itchy
So I'll probably avoid that too

I can't track tone or subtext
It's a weakness I've always had
You see it's a family thing
I inherited it from my dad

I wrote this poem at 3am
Curled up tight in my bed
I'll probably delete this later
These thoughts ought to stay in my head

This Is Not About Poetry

25

I only like the endings of poems
The beginning bores me to tears
I sometimes want to skip to the end
The middle bit drags on for years
I only like the ending of poems
But I do not wish to offend
Those who like reading the middle
I just want to know how it ends
Perhaps some great revelation
Or profound philosophical point
Or maybe it ends quite abruptly
And leaves you wondering

Alphabet Prayer

A prayer for the modern age
Because the old prayers
Can't really explain how
Dark the world feels to me
Every day
For without exaggeration I
Genuinely am worried that
Happiness no longer exists
In a way I can reach
Just like my grandparents thought but I
Know that it's true for me for
Love is a word that trips
My tongue like a
New-born foal taking its first steps
Or maybe I just need
Patience that the system will work as long as I
Quietly accept that the only
Real way I'll connect is through
Social media which though designed
To connect
Us has made the space so impossibly large that
all I can see is a gaping
Void and I'm still not convinced that there's
anyone out there
Who genuinely understands that if they

X-rayed my chest they'd find nothing but maybe
You see me or maybe you also
Zone out at parties

Mediocrity

In a rare moment of clarity
I confess with some hilarity
That my words hold no sincerity
And when I try for verity
It comes across vulgarity
And when speaking of posterity
I know that it is only charity
That allows for my mediocrity
To come across as wit

Emotional Support
Self-Deprecation

I cannot admit that I try
Because if I ever did
I would be admitting that my best was still not
Good.
I cannot ever care
Because if I ever did
I would be showing my heart could still be
Broken.
I cannot be excited
Because as soon as I do that
I know that I will be
Rejected.
So I will pretend that I don't care
That I never have to try
And when it all goes wrong at least
I saw it coming.

An Ode to Never Being Original

I can tell you nothing new under the sun
For those who first did see
Wrote of all the wonders of earth
And left nothing behind for me

I can tell you nothing new under the sun
For the dreamers that came before
Created entire new universes
And left no space for more

I can tell you nothing new under the sun
For great scientists already found
The secrets that life had hidden
Buried beneath the ground

I can tell you nothing new under the sun
For when the first lovers embraced
They inspired a million stories
So my version I misplaced

I can tell you nothing new under the sun
So you may ask, why do I write?
I am afraid you may have a point
And so I say goodnight